What if it Wasn't A Dream?

Mary C. Baumgartner

To order additional copies of this book, contact:
Xlibris
1-888-795-4274
www.Xlibris.com
Orders@Xlibris.com

ISBN:	Softcover	978-1-7960-8679-9
	Hardcover	978-1-7960-8680-5
	EBook	978-1-7960-8678-2

Library of Congress Control Number: 2020902461

Print information available on the last page.

Rev. date: 02/05/2020

Acknowledgements

This book is dedicated to my first Grandchild, Dexter Paul. I love him with all of my heart and want him to know I loved him before I even met him. He has changed my life and makes me so happy. I hope he always follows his dreams.

I want to thank my wonderful Daughter Grayce for her Illustrations; she made our book come alive. Without her this would not have been possible. Thank you Grayce for the many hours you spent to help make my dreams come true. I love you

I want to thank my family for always encouraging me to do something with my books. Thank you for believing in me.

I also want to thank the love of my life for believing in me and making me love myself. He makes me laugh and feel loved everyday. I thank God everyday for bringing him to me.

Lastly I am so thankful and believe dreams do come true. Always follow your dreams!

What If It Wasn't A Dream

What if the grass was a different
color than green?

What if it was the prettiest
color you had ever seen.

Maybe it would be pink, purple or red?

Whatever colors you could see in your head.

What if raindrops were lemonade and snow was ice cream? What if this was real and wasn't a dream?

What if fireflies were all
different colors at night?

Wouldn't that be a colorful sight?

12♥34

What if cars ran on juice instead of gas?

We could drive for hours and
let the time pass.

Hello!

What if animals could really talk? What if birds couldn't fly but could only walk?

What if clouds were fluffy and square?
Would people notice, would people care?

What if people were colors like
cinnamon, mocha and cream?

What if this was real and wasn't a dream?

What if in your garden cookies would grow?

Some would grow fast and
some would grow slow.

What if mud was chocolate
pudding that you could eat?
Wouldn't that be a tasty treat?

What if everyone knew how to read?
Books would grow by planting a seed.

What if money really did grow on trees?

What if everyone always said
Thank You and Please?

Grahm
06
Grayce
03

What if brother and sisters
never had a fight?

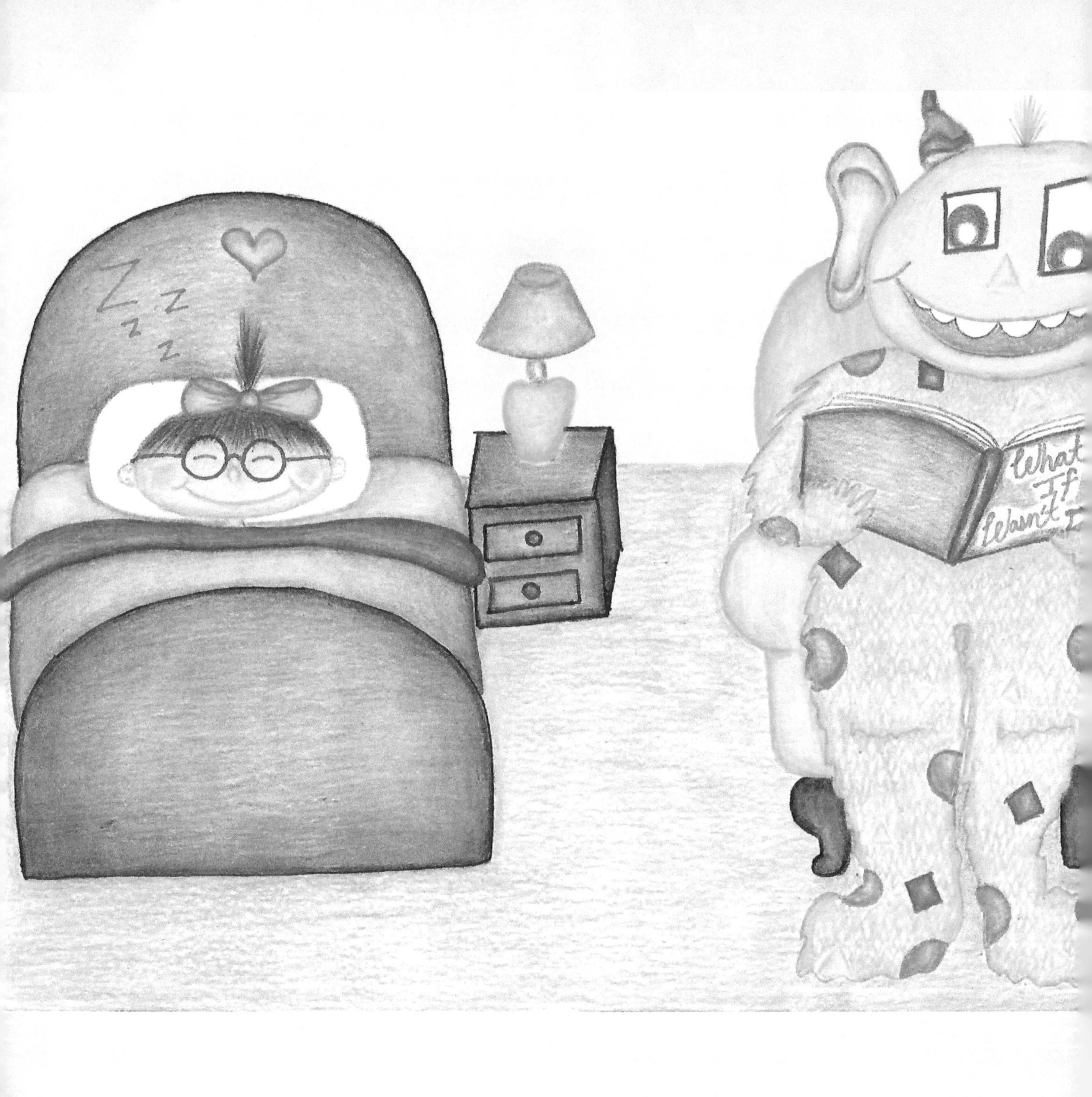
What
If
Wasn't

What if we weren't scared at night?

What if the sun was blue and
the moon was red?

What if we stayed up and
never went to bed?

What if feet always smelled
sweet and clean?

What if this was real and wasn't a dream?

What if best friends weren't hard to find?

What if school bullies weren't
mean but kind?

What if we always felt safe
and never afraid?

What if we never got hurt when we played?

What if everyone was always
trusting and kind?

What kind of a world do you
think we would find?

Goodnight

What if the moon winked
and said goodnight?

Then watched over you until
the morning light?

What if in your dreams the grass was
green and birds could fly and rain
and snow really fell from the sky?

Z
z
Z
z

What dream would you want to be true?

If it was all up to you?